Seeing with Your Fingers

Kids with Blindness and Visual Impairment

Kids with Special Needs

Seeing with Your Fingers:
Kids with Blindness and Visual Impairment

Listening with Your Eyes:
Kids Who Are Deaf and Hard of Hearing

My Name Is Not Slow:
Kids with Intellectual Disabilities

Sick All the Time: **Kids with Chronic Illness**

Something's Wrong!
Kids with Emotional Disturbance

Speed Racer: **Kids with Attention-Deficit/
Hyperactivity Disorder**

Finding My Voice: **Kids with Speech Impairment**

I Can Do It! **Kids with Physical Challenges**

The Hidden Child: **Kids with Autism**

What's Wrong with My Brain?
Kids with Brain Injury

Why Can't I Learn Like Everyone Else?
Kids with Learning Disabilities

Seeing with Your Fingers
Kids with Blindness and Visual Impairment

by Sheila Stewart and Camden Flath

MASON CREST PUBLISHERS INC.
370 Reed Road
Broomall, Pennsylvania 19008
(866)MCP-BOOK (toll free)
www.masoncrest.com

First Printing
9 8 7 6 5 4 3 2 1

ISBN (set) 978-1-4222-1727-6   ISBN (pbk set) 978-1-4222-1918-8

Library of Congress Cataloging-in-Publication Data

Stewart, Sheila, 1975–
  Seeing with your fingers : kids with blindness and visual impairment / by Sheila Stewart and Camden Flath.
      p. cm.
  Includes bibliographical references and index.
  ISBN 978-1-4222-1716-0   ISBN (pbk) 978-1-4222-1919-5
  1. Blind children—Juvenile literature. 2. Children with visual disabilities—Juvenile literature. 3. Blindness—Juvenile literature. I. Flath, Camden, 1987– II. Title.
  HV1596.3.S74 2010
  362.4'1083—dc22
                              2010005210

Produced by Harding House Publishing Service, Inc.
www.hardinghousepages.com
Design by MK Bassett-Harvey.
Cover design by Torque Advertising Design.
Printed in the USA by Bang Printing.

Photo Credits
Creative Commons Attribution 2.0 Generic: pg 33; Dreamstime: Brown, Paul Pg 28; Laures Pg 39; Lavrentev, Sergey Pg 43; Powers, Glenda Pg 26; Roberto1977 Pg 40; Sagynbaev, Nurbek pg 31; Syedumairhussain Pg 27; Tiplyashin, Anatoly Pg 37.

The creators of this book have made every effort to provide accurate information, but it should not be used as a substitute for the help and services of trained professionals.

Introduction

To the Teacher

Kids with Special Needs provides a unique forum for demystifying a wide variety of childhood medical and developmental disabilities. Written to captivate an elementary-level audience, the books bring to life the challenges and triumphs experienced by children with common chronic conditions such as hearing loss, intellectual disability, physical differences, and speech difficulties. The topics are addressed frankly through a blend of fiction and fact.

This series is particularly important today as the number of children with special needs is on the rise. Over the last two decades, advances in pediatric medical techniques have allowed children who have chronic illnesses and disabilities to live longer, more functional lives. At the same time, IDEA, a federal law, guarantees their rights to equal educational opportunities. As a result, these children represent an increasingly visible part of North American population in all aspects of daily life. Students are exposed to peers with special needs in their classrooms, through extracurricular activities, and in the community. Often, young people have misperceptions and unanswered questions about a child's disabilities—and more important, his or her abilities. Many times, there is no vehicle for talking about these complex issues in a comfortable manner.

This series will encourage further conversation about these issues. Most important, the series promotes a greater comfort for its readers as they live, play, and study side by side with these children who have medical and developmental differences—kids with special needs.

—*Dr. Carolyn Bridgemohan*
Boston Pediatric Hospital/Harvard Medical School

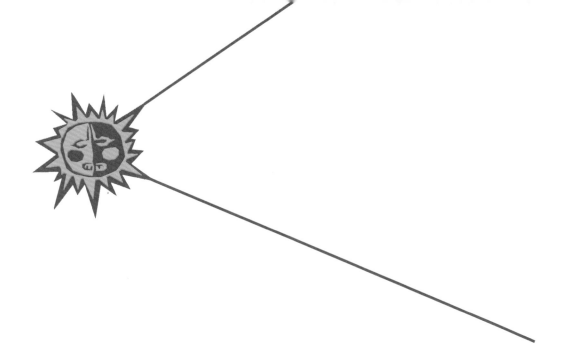

Miguel gripped the railing and slowly climbed the three steps to the front doors of the school, his other hand clutching his long white cane. He couldn't see his cane, of course, but he knew it was white. His white cane was what told the world he was blind.

Don't trip, don't trip. He sensed his dad just behind him, ready to steady him if he needed it.

It had been just over a year since the accident. The stupid accident that had taken his sight, leaving him with only a few dim shadows in his right eye and absolutely nothing in his left.

What he remembered most from the accident was horrible pain and the sound of his own screaming. He and his best friend Alex had been messing around in the backyard, trying to copy something they'd seen online. It had to do with putting a bottle rocket inside a glass bottle. Of course, on the videos they'd seen, nobody had gotten hurt. Miguel had known it was stupid, even at the time, but since then he'd heard a lot about just how stupid it had been. He wasn't sure what had gone wrong, but the bottle had exploded before he could turn away, spraying shards of glass across his face.

For a year, Miguel had been in rehab—learning to move around on his own, learning Braille, learning how to take care of himself without being able to

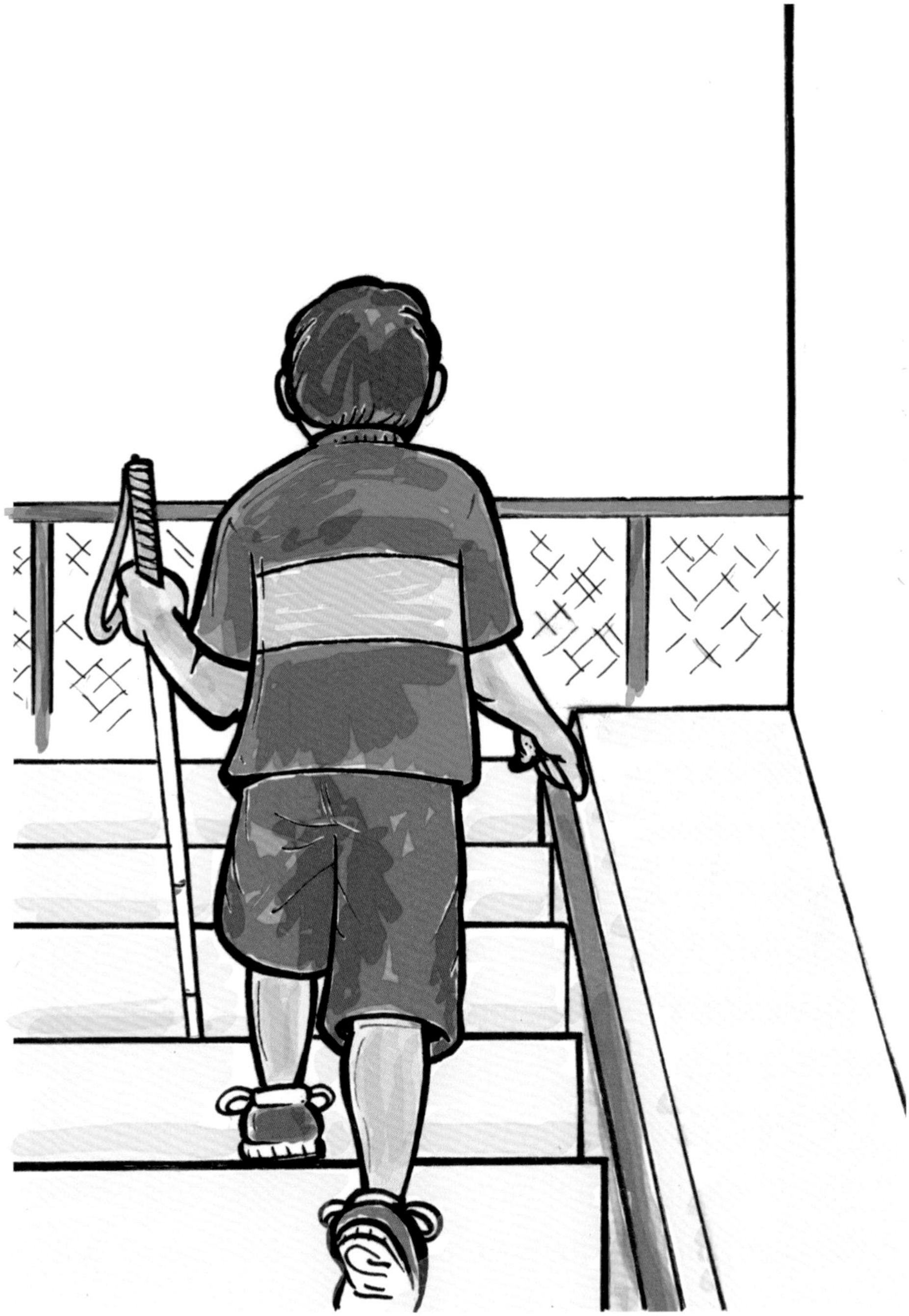

see his surroundings. He'd had tutors, to make sure he didn't get too far behind in class, but now he was going back to school again. Back to class with all the kids who had been his friends before the accident and who hadn't been around since.

Liz, who was going to be Miguel's aide, was waiting for him just inside the doors. Miguel smelled her perfume before she said anything—kind of a spicy-sweet scent. He liked that she wore it because he always knew when she was there. He'd been meeting with her now for a few weeks to get ready for the beginning of school.

"Are you feeling ready?" Liz asked.

He loved her voice, and he wished he knew what she looked like. He hadn't been blind long enough to stop wondering that kind of thing. He didn't know if he would ever stop wondering, though.

"I don't think I'll ever be ready," Miguel said. "I guess it might as well be now." He thought he sounded braver than he felt. That was good, since he felt sick to his stomach with dread.

Miguel's dad gave him a hug. "Have a good day," he said, his voice gruff. "I'm proud of you."

I wonder why he's proud of me. Miguel remembered his father screaming, "How could you be so stupid?" not long after the accident. It hadn't seemed then like he was very proud of him.

"Bye, Dad," Miguel said.

Liz bumped Miguel's shoulder with her elbow, to let him know where her arm was. He put his hand on her arm and they started down the hall to the classroom. They'd gotten to school early, since it was the first day, but soon Miguel would have to learn how to walk down the hall when it was crowded with other students.

In the classroom, Miguel sat at his desk, exploring it with his hands. Liz was setting out his things and telling him where they were.

"Your Brailler is directly in front of you," she said, "and your slate and stylus are in the top right corner, in case you need them."

Miguel reached out and lightly touched the typewriter-like machine with his fingers. He still wasn't very quick with Braille, but he was getting better.

"I've attached a folder of paper to the right side of your desk," Liz continued, and Miguel slid his hand over and felt the heavy sheets of Braille paper.

The classroom had been empty when Miguel and Liz had come in. Echoes had run around the room when they moved or talked. Now, other kids were starting to come in, filling up the echoes with their bodies.

Miguel could tell the moment someone noticed him. A couple of kids would be talking and laughing, and then they would suddenly stop, their voices would drop to whispers or murmurs. Miguel might not be able to see, but he knew people were staring at him.

"Okay, Miguel," Liz said. "For the most part, I'm going to let you work on your own. I'll be sitting at a table to your left, though, if you need me, and I'll check in with you from time to time."

"Welcome to sixth grade," a woman at the front of the room said. "I'm Mrs. Blake."

Miguel was very aware of the students sitting around him. Because it was the first day of school, they weren't doing much real work. Mrs. Blake had everyone introduce themselves, but a lot of the kids mumbled their names so quickly that Miguel couldn't understand them. He thought the girl in front of him was named Kate, and the boy right behind him was Joe or Joel or something like that. He thought he heard Alex's voice, too, somewhere on the other side of the room. Alex had been his best friend since kindergarten, but he hadn't been around at all since the accident.

Miguel pulled his Brailler closer to him and fed in a piece of paper. He felt like everyone was watching him, but he tried to ignore the feeling. He was going to have to get used to this, but everyone else was going to have to get used to him, too. He pushed the keys to spell out, "Mrs. Blake is my teacher. Kate

sits in front of me. Joe sits behind me. Alex is in this class, too."

Mrs. Blake started talking about the things they were going to learn that year and Miguel tried to take notes. He got behind almost right away. While he was still struggling to type out, "We will learn about the solar system," Mrs. Blake had moved on to, "We'll also be talking about issues that affect our world today." This was going to be hard.

In the afternoon, Miguel's class went to the playground. Miguel sat on the ground near the school building, feeling the breeze on his face and listening to the other kids playing. He could hear a basketball being dribbled, and kids laughing and shouting. He remembered when he had been one of them. He would probably have been playing basketball with Alex and a couple of the other guys. Or maybe they would have been swinging from hand to hand on the monkey bars, pretending to be monkeys. *Or are we too old for that now?* he wondered. The world had gone on without him and he didn't even know what the other kids would be doing now.

Suddenly, something hit his knee. He put out his hand and touched it. A ball. He picked it up, but he didn't know which direction he should throw it back.

"Hey, No-Eyes!" someone yelled. "Hand over the ball!"

No-Eyes? Great. He threw the ball toward the voice, but he must have thrown badly, because he heard laughter and snickering.

"Shut up!" somebody else yelled. "Leave him alone!"

Was that Alex's voice? He wasn't sure. He wanted it to be Alex, but what he really wanted was for Alex to still be his friend. For things to be like they used to be, before the accident.

At home that night, Miguel didn't feel like eating. He picked at his mom's baked macaroni and cheese, stabbing pieces with his fork and nibbling at them.

His sister Dani was excited about being in eleventh grade, and she chattered on about the kids in her class, what everyone had worn for the first day of school and what boys had gotten cuter over the summer.

Miguel wasn't really listening to Dani, but when she suddenly stopped talking, he wondered what had just happened. It took a lot to shut Dani up.

"I want to hear more about your day, Miguel," Mom said. He'd told them it wasn't great, but he hadn't felt like talking much when he got home from school.

He shrugged. "I think Alex is in my class—but I'm not sure."

"Mrs. Blake told me she was going to make sure everyone told you their names," Dad said, "so that you'd know who was in your class."

"Yeah, well, it was kind of hard to tell what everyone said. Plus, you know, it's not like I can just know everyone by their voice right away." He took a bite, then added, "Somebody called me No-Eyes."

Miguel hadn't expected the reaction his family would have to the "No-Eyes" comment. Mom had burst into tears, which was awful. Dani had gotten angry and said she wanted to come by the next day to see who was being mean to her little brother. Dad had been angry too, but then he had said, "This kind of thing is going to happen, Miguel. People can be really cruel."

Mom had wanted to call the principal and Mrs. Blake and Liz, but Dad had talked her down to just Mrs. Blake and Liz, and he had made her wait until she calmed down.

Mom was stubborn and there wasn't any way Miguel could talk her out of calling. He went into the living room while she called his teacher. He figured it was something she needed to do to make herself feel better, but he didn't want to listen to the conversation. He turned on the TV and listened to the voices. He tried to figure out what was going on, but it was confusing. A few shows were available with descriptive video service, where someone described what the people on screen were doing, but most shows didn't have it.

He wished he didn't have to go back to school. He'd be happier not being there, and everyone else would be just as happy he wasn't there, too.

"We're going to do a special project today," Mrs. Blake announced at the beginning of class the next day. "It's an art project, so we'll be working on it in the art room."

An art project? Miguel thought. *Great, pick something where you have to use your eyes.*

"This project will be a little different, though," Mrs. Blake continued. "I know you are all very aware that we have a student in class who can't see. For this project, we will be exploring what it is like to be blind."

Miguel felt his face get hot, but he was curious now to know more about the project.

"You will be using clay to make sculptures of each other's faces. But the trick is, you have to do it without using your eyes. You will wear blindfolds, and you will only be allowed to see with your fingers, not your eyes. Everyone pick a partner, and we'll go down to the art room and get started."

The class all started talking at once. People were standing up and moving around. Miguel sat still, waiting for Liz to come and help him find his way to the art room. He wasn't sure what he thought about this.

"Hey Miguel," someone said. "Do you want to be my partner?"

"Alex?" Miguel asked. Then, because he was afraid Alex might change his mind, he said quickly, "Yeah, sure, let's be partners."

He found his white cane and stood up. He knew Liz was there, because he could smell her perfume, but she let him find his own way around his desk.

"Do you want to hold my arm?" Alex asked.

"Um, ok." He took Alex's arm and they walked to the art room. They didn't say anything, but that was okay.

In the art room, Mrs. Blake gave everyone a lump of clay and passed out blindfolds to everyone except Miguel.

"Now," said Mrs. Blake, "I want you to take turns using your fingers to see what your partner's face looks like. If the blindfold is in the way, you can move it to see your partner's eyes, but make sure you don't cheat and use your own eyes. And no messing around or you'll have to make your sculpture of me instead."

Miguel reached out his hand slowly toward Alex. People were giggling and talking, but he felt nervous. His hand bumped into Alex's chest and he raised it to touch his face. He'd explored his family's faces like this, but Alex was different. Touching someone's face was personal, and he hadn't talked to Alex in over a year. He brushed his fingers over Alex's cheeks and nose and up to his eyes and then stopped. Alex's eyes were wet, like he was crying.

"I'm sorry, Miguel," Alex whispered. "I'm really, really sorry."

For a second, Miguel didn't know what to say. Then he put his hands on Alex's shoulders and said, "I still want to be friends, Alex. I miss you."

They stood there like that for a few minutes and then went back to their project. Miguel let Alex touch his face and then they both worked on their clay.

"This is hard," Alex said. "I'm going to make you look like a lumpy potato. Sorry, man."

"Well, you'll have to tell me what I make you look like," Miguel said.

At the end of the class, Mrs. Blake told everyone to take off their blindfolds and look at their sculptures. There was a lot of laughing as the kids looked at each other's work.

"Yep, pretty much a lumpy potato," Alex said, and guided Miguel's hands so he could feel Alex's sculpture of him.

"Uh, Alex? Where's my nose?" Miguel asked. Alex's sculpture didn't even feel much like a face.

Alex wasn't listening. "Wow, Miguel, this is great!"

he said. "It actually kind of looks like me. A little any-way. Hey, come look at this," he called to someone else.

Soon, the class was gathering around to see Miguel's sculpture.

"Cool!" someone said. "I wish I could do that. Will you teach me, Miguel?"

Miguel wished he could see what he'd made, but he smiled. He felt like part of the class again, and that was a good feeling.

Kids and Visual Impairment

About 12 out of every 1000 kids has some type of visual *impairment*. This means that there is some problem with their ability to see clearly. Blindness is when a person has a total loss of vision. There are many, many disorders that cause visual impairments and many different levels of sight among the visually impaired.

> An *impairment* is a handicap or something that makes things that are normally easy more difficult.

Children who have visual impairments might have blurry vision or be unable to see things clearly that are far away. A kid with a visual impairment may not be able to read the white board in class or see clearly the face of a person talking to them. They might not be able to see at all. Sometimes visual impairments are easy to correct, and glasses or contact lenses make all the difference. Sometimes a problem

Some kinds of visual impairment can be corrected easily with glasses or contact lenses.

SIDE VIEW OF EYE

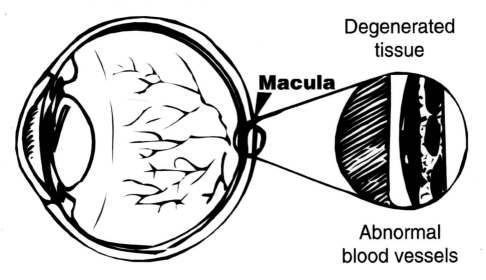

Degenerated tissue

Macula

Abnormal blood vessels

cannot be corrected, and a person must change many parts of his life in order to do his best.

Think about how important your sense of sight can be. We need sight to talk, move around, and learn about our world. Students who are blind or have visual impairments not only have to learn the same things students who can see clearly do, but they must learn without the aid of sight.

There are many difficulties children with visual impairment or blindness face, but there are also many ways these students can succeed in and out of school. There are also many ways kids who are not visually impaired can help students who are. Ultimately, blindness or visual impairment is just one part of who a person is. Kids who can see clearly and kids with visual impairments are the same in many more ways than they are different.

What Is Visual Impairment?

The phrase "visual impairment" describes many types of vision problems, from blurry vision to blindness, rather than any one disease or disorder. Visual impairment is simply the loss of some or all vision.

Schools use several terms to describe different degrees of visual impairment. These descriptions are based on

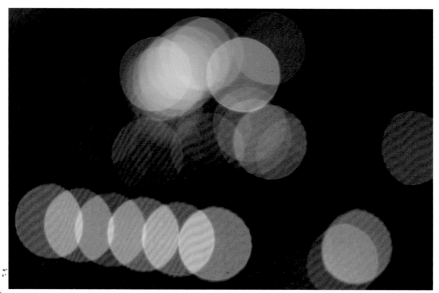

Visual impairment can make things look blurry or out of focus.

the Snellen eye chart. In the Snellen system, 20/20 vision is perfect. This means that a person can read what most people can read at 20 feet away from an eye chart. 20/200 vision means that a person must be standing 20 feet away from the chart to read what most people can read at 200 feet away.

Visual impairment is often broken down into the following *categories*:

1. **Partially sighted:** Partially sighted means that because of a problem with their vision, a student needs either special education or changes in the classroom to help them learn most efficiently.

2. **Low vision:** Students with low vision have difficulty seeing clearly either close-up or far away even with glasses or contact lenses. These students will need special tools to help them in school, including books on tape, computers with bigger letters, and special lights.

> *Categories* are groups of a certain kind of thing; a way to sort things into groups.

3. **Legally blind:** To be considered legally blind, a student's vision must be less than 20/200 on the Snellen eye chart system while using glasses or contact lenses. Students who are legally blind need the same sorts

of classroom materials that students with low vision do, but they also might benefit from learning Braille. Braille is a system of reading by touch developed to help the blind communicate.

4. **Totally blind:** If a student is totally blind, she must use Braille to read, as well as other nonvisual ways of learning in school.

How Does the Eye Work?

The eye is a very complicated organ. It has many parts, and each part is important to our ability to see. If something is wrong with any of these parts, it can cause a visual impairment or blindness.

Parts of the eye:

- **Sclera:** The sclera is the white part of your eye. This firm outer layer protects the inside of the eye.
- **Cornea:** The cornea covers the front part of the eye and helps your eye focus.
- **Iris:** The iris is the colored part of your eye. It can be blue, green, brown, or a combination of those colors.
- **Pupil:** The pupil is the black part in the center of the eye. It changes size to allow less or more light into the eye.
- **Lens:** The lens focuses light coming into the eye onto the retina.

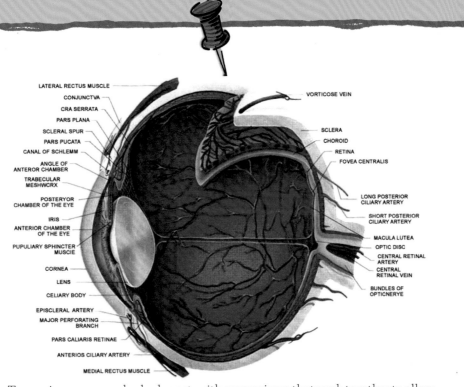

LATERAL RECTUS MUSCLE
CONJUNCTVA
CRA SERRATA
PARS PLANA
SCLERAL SPUR
PARS PUCATA
CANAL OF SCHLEMM
ANGLE OF ANTEROR CHAMBER
TRABECULAR MESHWCRX
POSTERYOR CHAMBER OF THE EYE
IRIS
ANTERIOR CHAMBER OF THE EYE
PUPULIARY SPHINCTER MUSCIE
CORNEA
LENS
CELIARY BODY
EPISCLERAL ARTERY
MAJOR PERFORATING BRANCH
PARS CALIARIS RETINAE
ANTERIOS CILIARY ARTERY
MEDIAL RECTUS MUSCLE

VORTICOSE VEIN
SCLERA
CHOROID
RETINA
FOVEA CENTRALIS
LONG POSTERIOR CILIARY ARTERY
SHORT POSTERIOR CILIARY ARTERY
MACULA LUTEA
OPTIC DISC
CENTRAL RETINAL ARTERY
CENTRAL RETINAL VEIN
BUNDLES OF OPTICNERYE

The eye is a very complex body part, with many pieces that work together to allow us to see.

- **Retina:** Light coming into the eye is focused on the retina, which turns it into electrical signals to send to the brain. The retina is what lets you see light and dark, as well as colors.

- **Macula:** The macula is the part of the retina that sees *details* best.

> *Details are the little parts of something.*

- **Optic nerve:** The optic nerve carries electrical signals to the brain so that your brain can make sense of them. Even if the rest of your eye works perfectly, if the message doesn't get to your brain, you won't be able to see.

How do each of these parts help your eyes to see? First, light enters the eye through the cornea, then passes through the pupil, and finally, into the lens. Muscles change the shape of the lens to focus light on the retina, where images and light are changed into electrical signals by special cells called **cones** and **rods**. The optic nerve then sends these electrical signals to the brain. The brain is where the signals sent through the optic nerve from the retina are formed into the images that make up what you see.

Cones are cone-shaped cells in the retina that respond to color, light, and detail. Cone cells are far more sensitive than rod cells.

Rods are long cells in the retina that react to light. They allow for side and night vision. There are many more rod cells than cone cells.

What Causes Visual Impairment or Blindness?

Different problems can damage your eye's ability to see clearly. Certain sicknesses or accidents that damage the eye can cause visual impairment. Some people are also born blind or with visual impairment.

Low vision can make recognizing faces much more difficult.

Macular Degeneration

Macular degeneration is a condition where the macula breaks down, making it difficult, or even impossible to see clearly. Young people sometimes get a type of macular degeneration called macular dystrophy.

Retinal Detachment

Retinal detachment is when the retina is separated from its blood supply, causing a loss of vision in that area of the eye. Retinal detachment in children is often caused by an accident that damages the eye. Detachment of the retina can only be fixed by surgery.

Other Eye Disorders

Other eye disorders that can cause visual impairment include **cataracts**, **glaucoma**, **diabetes**, and some infections. Children don't usually become blind through these conditions.

Many other problems with the way light is **refracted** inside the eye can cause issues with vision. Many of these problems can be corrected with glasses or contact lenses. They include:

- **Myopia:** Also known as nearsightedness, myopia makes far-away images to look blurry. Myopia is caused by the light being focused in front of the retina, rather than directly on it.

- **Hyperopia:** This condition is also called farsightedness. It can make things that are close-up look blurry, and even cause pain in the eye.

- **Astigmatism:** This problem with the eye's cornea causes blurry vision, mostly of lines.

Cataracts make the lens of your eye become foggy.

Glaucoma increases the pressure inside your eye, making it hard to see.

Diabetes interferes with your body's ability to process sugar normally, which can cause blindness.

When light is refracted, it is bent, as happens when light passes through a lens, a piece of glass, or water.

- **Presbyopia:** This condition makes it hard to focus on things that are close to you. It is caused by a hardening of the lens of the eye, usually as a person gets older.

Who Cares for Your Eyes?

Many *professionals* work to care for your eyes, *diagnosing* and treating problems that can have a *negative* effect on vision. These doctors and *specialists* are the people working to make sure you can see clearly and without trouble.

Ophthalmologists are doctors who specialize in the eye. They understand its *anatomy*, how it works to allow you to see, and the issues that can cause trouble with people's sight. Ophthalmologists are experts in the many diseases and disorders that can affect the eye, cause

Professionals are people who are trained to do a specific job for which they are paid.

Diagnosing means discovering what sickness or disorder a person has.

Something that is *negative* is harmful or bad.

Specialists are people who are trained to be very good at one particular thing (such as a doctor who is trained to treat only eyes).

Anatomy is the way something is made.

visual impairment, or even blindness. Some of these eye doctors *specialize* in specific parts of the eye. Retinal specialists, for example, are ophthalmologists who work on the retina, and understand the diseases that can harm it.

Optometrists are doctors who specialize in the disorders and diseases that can harm vision or the eye. They test patients for nearsightedness, farsightedness, astigmatism, presbyopia, and many other disorders. Optometrists *prescribe* glasses, contact lenses, medicines, and many other treatments for disorders of the eye.

> To *specialize* means to be trained to be very good at one particular thing or in one particular area.
>
> To *prescribe* means to tell a person to do something (or take something) as treatment for a medical condition.

Opticians then sell glasses prescribed by optometrists. They cannot make prescriptions, but opticians help in treating problems of the eye with eyeglasses.

Protecting Your Vision

Eye experts believe that one thing you can do to take care of your vision is to eat a healthy diet. Eating a balanced diet can prevent many problems with sight that can develop later in life. Doctors and scientists suggest that a diet of leafy vegetables, fruits, and at least two servings of fish per week can help keep your eyes healthy. By avoiding fatty snack foods, you can do your part in preventing vision problems.

Smoking is also bad for your eyes, and it can even cause blindness. Don't start smoking, and you'll be doing your eyes (and the rest of your body) a favor!

Aids for Visual Impairment

For many vision problems, glasses, medicine, or surgery can help. Many refraction problems can be corrected with glasses or contact lenses, for example. If students still have trouble reading, recognizing faces, or seeing clearly,

Contact lenses help many people with refraction problems to see clearly.

they may be experiencing issues related to low vision.

Low vision is also known as usable vision. Doctors such as ophthalmologists and optometrists work to diagnose the individual needs of students with low vision. They can decide on the best tools to help a student in the classroom and at home.

There are many things kids, parents, and teachers can do to help students with low vision. Large-print materials such as clocks, books, and calculators can be a big help in school. Computer screens can be magnified to aid those with low vision, as well. Sometimes doctors suggest that learning and using Braille in schools can help students who have low vision.

Researchers and doctors are also working to find new treatments for those with limited vision or visual impairment. These new treatments include:

- retinal cell *transplants*
- retinal *microchip* implants, sometimes called a "bionic eye"
- *gene therapy*

Researchers are people who do experiments and study the results.

Transplants are when body parts from one person are put into another person.

A *microchip* is a tiny computer that replaces or helps a body part.

Gene therapy involves trying to change a person's DNA to solve problems related to health.

For students with low vision, changing the learning environment can be an important step toward success in school. New learning materials specifically made for these students are available and can make a big difference in a student's ability to do their best.

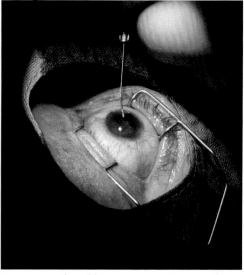

Some visual problems may require surgery.

Braille: Reading with Your Fingertips

Braille is a way for blind or visually impaired people to read using their fingertips. Braille is a language organized into "cells" or sets of raised dots on a piece of paper. Letters, numbers, words, and even punctuation marks are made with combinations of these small, raised bumps.

Louis Braille created Braille in 1820. Louis was a blind teenager living in Paris, France, when he changed a messaging system intended for the military into a way for him to read by touching bumps on paper. Braille allowed Louis and his friends at the National Institute for Blind Youth in Paris to read faster than they could with raised printed letters.

Today, Braille is used by many blind and visually impaired kids to read and communicate. There are two kinds of Braille.

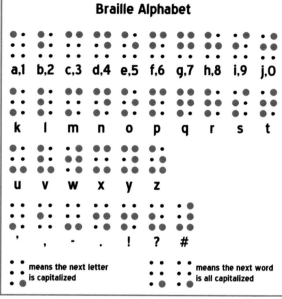

Braille Alphabet

a,1 b,2 c,3 d,4 e,5 f,6 g,7 h,8 i,9 j,0

k l m n o p q r s t

u v w x y z

' , - . ! ? #

means the next letter is capitalized

means the next word is all capitalized

In Braille, letters and symbols are made up of different combinations of raised bumps.

Grade 1

In Grade 1 Braille, every letter of every word is spelled out with Braille cells. Grade 1 Braille is slower to read because it is longer.

Grade 2

Grade 2 Braille is a system that needs fewer Braille bumps to communicate. Shortened forms of words and **contractions** are used in Grade 2 Braille to speed up reading. The most common kind of Braille, Grade 2 Braille has 76 shortened words and 189 different letter contractions.

Contractions are shortened forms of words. "Don't" is a contraction of "do not," for example, and "I'm" is a contraction of "I am."

40

Visual Impairment and Blindness in School

It is important for young people with visual impairments and partial or total blindness to get an accurate diagnosis as early as possible. Many children live for years without being tested for visual impairment. Not being able to see can make it harder for them to learn, communicate, and get along with others. Early diagnosis of vision problems allows kids and their families to get help from schools and doctors.

Classifies means to put something in a certain category.

Special education teaches kids who have trouble learning because of some disability.

To *qualify* means to fit the definition of something or to meet the requirements.

Once the school *classifies* a child as having a visual impairment, the school will begin making changes in the child's education. A law known as the Individuals with Disabilities Education Act, or IDEA, describes how schools decide which kids need *special education*. In order to *qualify* for IDEA, the child's condition must get in the way of him learning or taking part in school activities.

The IDEA law lists thirteen different kinds of *disabilities* that may mean a child will need special education. Blindness and visual impairment is one category that falls under IDEA.

The IDEA law requires that:

- the child has problems performing well at school activities.
- the child's parent, teacher, or other school staff person must ask that the child be examined for a disability.
- the child is *evaluated* to decide if she does indeed have a disability and to figure out what kind of special education she needs.
- a group of people, including the kid's parents, teachers, and a school psychologist, meets to decide on a plan for helping him (or her). This plan is called an Individualized Education Program (IEP). The IEP spells out exactly what the child needs in order to succeed at school.

Disabilities are problems—either physical or mental—that get in the way of a person doing what other people can do.

When something is *evaluated*, it is examined to see in which category it belongs.

Many schools have programs made especially for kids with visual impairment or blindness. Changes to learning materials in the classroom help students with partial sight or low vision learn to better use the sight they do have. Large-print books, books on tape, or magnifying tools can also help. Students who are blind can be helped by

Braille is a language that can be "read" by touching raised bumps on a page.

learning Braille when they are young. They may also need to learn better communication, new ways to get around, and skills for daily life in school and at home.

Computers allow many kids who are blind and visually impaired to take part in many of the class activities that they might not have in the past. As *technology* improves, many *electronic* methods for students with visual impairments are becoming more common. These electronic tools are breaking down some of the differences between blind, visually impaired, and sighted students.

Technology has to do with the machines and equipment made from new scientific research.

Electronic means that something works by using electricity.

Kids with visual impairment or blindness can also have fun doing the same kinds of games and sports that other kids can. Adapting sports for the safety of the visually impaired might mean using a ball that makes an electronic beep sound, for example. Many board games come with

> *Challenges* **are things a person finds difficult.**

special playing pieces and boards made for the visually impaired or blind. The *challenges* of blindness and visual impairment are often great, but those challenges can be overcome in many ways, so that the blind, visually impaired, and sighted can have fun and learn together.

Succeeding with Visual Impairment

Blind and visually impaired kids can achieve amazing things in and out of the classroom. Blindness or visual impairment may change the way a child experiences the world, but it is only one part of who he is. He can be a friend, student, athlete—just like any other kid.

More and more, students who are blind and visually impaired have new ways to succeed in school, on the playground, and at home. Computer technology, special classrooms or schools, and research being done on new treatments—are all allowing blind and visually impaired kids to get an education, make friends, and have fun.

Further Reading

Alexander, S. H. *Do You Remember the Color Blue? The Questions Kids Ask About Blindness*. New York: Viking, 2000.

Glasser, E. A. and M. Burgio. *All Children Have Different Eyes: Learn to Play and Make Friends*. Whittier, Calif.: Vidi Press, 2007.

Holbrook, M. C. *Children with Visual Impairments: A Guide for Parents*. Bethesda, Ma.: Woodbine House, 2006.

Koenig, A. and C. Holbrook. *Experiencing Literacy: A Parent's Guide for Fostering Literacy Development of Children with Visual Impairments*. Philadelphia, Penn.: Towers Press, 2005.

McLinden, M. *Learning Through Touch: Supporting Children with Visual Impairments and Additional Difficulties*. London: David Fulton Publishers, 2002.

Runyan, M. and S. Jenkins. *No Finish Line: My Life As I See It*. New York: Penguin Putnam, 2001.

Smith, K. *Dottie and Dots See Animal Spots: Learning Braille with Dots and Dottie*. Lincoln, Neb.: IUniverse, 2007.

Weihenmayer, E. *Touch the Top of the World: A Blind Man's Journey to Climb Farther than the Eye Can See*. New York: Penguin, 2001.

Find Out More On the Internet

American Council of the Blind
www.acb.org

Foundation Fighting Blindness
www.blindness.org

Lighthouse International
www.lighthouse.org

National Braille Press
www.nbp.org

National Dissemination Center for Children with Disabilities
(NICHCY)
www.nichcy.org

National Eye Institute
www.nei.nih.gov

National Federation of the Blind
www.nfb.org

The New York Institute for Special Education/Education of the
Blind (NYISE)
www.nyise.org

Prevent Blindness America
www.preventblindness.org

Disclaimer

Index

About the Authors

Sheila Stewart has written several dozen books for young people, both fiction and nonfiction, although she especially enjoys writing fiction. She has a master's degree in English and now works as a writer and editor. She lives with her two children in a house overflowing with books, in the Southern Tier of New York State.

Camden Flath is a writer living and working in Binghamton, New York. He has a degree in English and has written several books for young people. He is interested in current political, social, and economic issues and applies those interests to his writing.

About the Consultant

Dr. Carolyn Bridgemohan is board certified in developmental behavioral pediatrics and practices at the Developmental Medicine Center at Children's Hospital Boston. She is the director of the Autism Care Program and an assistant professor at Harvard Medical School. Her specialty areas are autism and other pervasive developmental disorders, developmental and learning problems, and developmental and behavioral pediatrics.